# FIFTY WAYS TO PERSONAL DEVELOPMENT

*Andrew Forrest*

*The Industrial Society*

First published in 1995 by
The Industrial Society
Robert Hyde House
48 Bryanston Square
London W1H 7LN
Telephone: 0171-262-2401


© *The Industrial Society 1995*


ISBN 1 85835 239 8


**British Library Cataloguing-in-Publication Data.**
**A Catalogue record for this book is available from the**
**British Library.**

Reprinted 1996, 1997, 1998, 1999.
737pub5.99

Typeset by: Midlands Book Typesetting
Printed by: Optichrome Ltd.
Cover Design: Rhodes Design


The Industry Society is a Registered
Charity No. 290003

# Acknowledgements

To Yael Bendahan, Chris Curtiss, Liz Upstone and Mairi Sudding for research and keyboard skills; to *People Management* magazine for several examples quoted in the text; and John Herring, Customer Account Manager at Dowty Aerospace Landing Gear Ltd for his contribution on Outdoors Training.

# Contents

## Section F Creative Skills

## Section G Build Up Contacts

## Section H Develop Others

## Appendix

# Introduction

This book is intended to stimulate anyone who is interested in personal development, whatever your occupation. While some of the methods described, such as a business game (No. 14), require the resources of an employer, many others do not, and if you are a student or unemployed you may be eligible for grants to assist your learning.

The book aims to show that many of us limit the scope of our own learning:

- by being unaware of our learning style (No. 36)
- by not using all four quadrants as learning opportunities (No. 19)
- by not distinguishing between knowledge, skills and behaviour (No. 1)
- by regarding learning as only "being sent on a course" (No. 17).

Because training courses are still the most familiar vehicles for learning, I have not included separate descriptions of the various techniques used on courses such as role-plays, brainstorming, in-tray exercises, etc.

Learning at work is currently receiving a surge of attention, and for two main reasons. First, the concept of the learning organisation, combining corporate learning – the readiness and ability of the organisation to learn from its collective experience – and individual learning on a lifelong multi-faceted basis, has gained significant ground. Second, flatter organisation structures now mean significantly less vertical promotion. So people who want career progression are looking for new ways to keep fresh, to broaden their knowledge and to contribute beyond their original specialism.

I do not for a moment expect anyone to use all fifty of the methods in this book. You can pick and choose as you wish; but I would make two suggestions. First, if you keep a learning log (No. 4) your learning will become cumulative, as one method reinforces another. Second, from time to time check whether your learning is lopsided. Are you concentrating too much on one cluster of methods (e.g. creative skills) to the detriment of another (e.g. group work)?

The gradual compilation of these fifty ways of personal development has been achieved through the enthusiasm of various groups of managers over a ten-year period. These include civil servants in Scotland, printing industry managers in London, personnel managers in Worcester and health service managers in Birmingham. They have brainstormed and tried out the fifty methods, and I thank them most warmly.

# 1

# Develop your Learning Skills

It is extraordinary, but true, that most of us have never been taught how to learn. We have worked out for ourselves how to take notes, and generally acquired a rather passive approach to our development, waiting to be sent on training courses which someone else has decided will be good for us.

The approach called self-managed learning is dealt with in No. 15. But first, some suggestions on how to sharpen up your personal ability to learn.

It helps to differentiate between knowledge, skills and behaviour. If you are acquiring knowledge, i.e. facts, you need to get them "right first time", otherwise you become confused and your brain has to unlearn inaccurate knowledge before replacing it with the correct version. Facts simply have to be memorised.

1

But learning a skill is different. Skills require practice, and (within sensible safety limits) trial and error can actually be a good way of learning. In learning to drive a car, we have to memorise road signs and the rules of the Highway Code (knowledge), but I can still remember my driving instructor helping me to learn gentle adjustments to the clutch (skill) by saying "up the thickness of a penny, down the thickness of a penny". This is why pilots learn how to fly jumbo jets using simulators before trying the real thing!

Learning to change your behaviour is different again. A person whose behaviour is unacceptable, e.g. racist or sexist, will only learn to change if you make an impact both on their reasoning and their emotion.

If you have never explored your natural learning style, see No. 36 for a description of a useful questionnaire. And whatever your style, you may be able significantly to improve your retention of new learning by:

- increasing your reading speed (see No. 2)
- using aids to note-taking; pattern notes ("spider diagrams") replicate the networks within the brain and help your memory
- using mnemonics (turning the initial letters of a sequence which you need to remember into a memorable phrase, e.g. the five essentials for setting up a learning resource centre are Commitment, Rationale, Advertising, Site, Help = CRASH).

See the Resources section for books by Tony Buzan and others on this theme.

# 2

# Guided Reading

Guided reading means purposeful and sustained reading, with advice from a tutor or expert. This advice may include helping you to select a particular theme within a subject which interests you, and guiding you towards appropriate books or sources. For instance, if you are considering setting up your own business and want to know more about management in retailing, a tutor could steer you towards books about retailing in general; biographies of effective retailers like Anita Roddick; journals specialising in retailing, such as *Retail Week* and *The Grocer* and surveys such as Mintel and Verdict.

Many people lose the habit of purposeful reading when they finish their full-time education, and it can seem a chore to restart, particularly in the face of competition from other media, such as television, which require less personal effort. So here are three suggestions:

- Ease yourself back into the reading habit by first tackling articles and paperbacks rather than formidable hardbacks.
- Spruce up your reading speed. A booklet on rapid reading, or a short course, can work wonders. Indeed, what you understand and retain from reading may well increase rather than diminish by reading more quickly.
- It may be better to read three books of 150 pages rather than one of 450 pages: the length of a book does not necessarily guarantee its quality. There is arguably more skill in refining a subject down to a few chapters than in rambling on self-indulgently.

You can use your guided reading to increase your knowledge; to gain ideas or stimulus; or to develop new ways of looking at things. If your aim is to acquire more knowledge, consider just how much detail you need to remember – it may be just a few key points. Mastering how to use sources of reference, so that you can quickly find what you need to know, may be more useful than absorbing a lot of superfluous information.

An essential part of your guided reading programme should be to familiarise yourself with a good library, and its cataloguing systems. Libraries are increasingly computerised, so it may help to ask one of the staff to guide you if you are not up to scratch.

Guided reading does not limit you to books. All manner of publications are available, including national newspapers, trade journals, reports, articles.

# 3

# Write a Report Summary or Book Review

This involves being able to summarise a long document, such as a book or major report, and to present it accurately, making a clear distinction between factual summary and your own comment. At work, senior managers typically have to read a great many lengthy reports, so they value someone with the ability to condense these into their key points. These often form an "Executive summary" at the front of the report. Developing the ability to summarise also will increase your reading speed (see No. 2), because you will be searching for the salient points and skimming the incidental material.

Separating facts from opinion is notoriously difficult. C. P. Scott, a great editor of the *Manchester Guardian*, used to tell his journalists, "Comment is free, but facts are sacred". One way of improving this skill is to read a report, article or book by someone with whom you disagree; then to produce a clinically fair summary of their arguments (facts) before demolishing them with your own views (comment)!

At school, you may not have relished those English lessons where the teacher asked you to write a précis: reducing yards of prose to a few crisp sentences. Years later as an adult, however, you may wish that you had perfected the talent – but it is never too late to learn.

One way of honing this skill is to select a subject which you find interesting and offer to review books on this subject for your local newspaper. You may be rationed to 100 or 200 words, so it provides a good test of your self-discipline. (You also get to keep the book!)

# 4

# Keeping a "Learning Log"

Each of us learns in our own way (see No. 36). A powerful aid to your learning is a personal log. This usually takes the form of a loose-leaf binder divided into several sections. One section holds any official documents related to your training or qualifications, such as certificates, diplomas, etc. Another is allocated for your personal development plan or learning contract (see No. 38). At your regular discussions with your manager, you review progress towards your plan and update it.

A third section allows room for your own notes about your learning experiences. This is like a private diary, and you are under no obligation to show these notes to anyone. It helps your learning if you make entries in this section on a "little and often" basis, so that you can record how you feel at the time.

If you make frequent short entries and review them at intervals, you will gain confidence in your learning. It will allow you to look back and see that what was difficult two months ago is easier now. Or, if it is not improving, you can discuss the evidence with your manager or a tutor. If you have a mentor (see No. 34), you may well find the log also produces part of the agenda for your meetings.

As well as recording incidents in your own learning, you may want to include a section on what you are doing to help others to learn – e.g. if you are asked to run a training session or coach a colleague.

# 5

# Listen to Cassette Tapes "on the Move"

Increased awareness of time management has contributed to the growth of this method of self-development.

With the aid of the personal stereo, study cassettes can be used in your car or on public transport. Broadly speaking there are three types:

- languages
- a lecture on a theme, such as delegation
- a debate or round-table discussion with a group of experts.

Language tapes help you not only to acquire knowledge – the meaning of the words – but also skill in their pronunciation. They usually include gaps that allow you to practise saying the word out loud. For this reason use in your own car is more popular than public transport! You will obviously need conversational practice to reinforce your learning, but tapes can provide a valuable beginning.

A taped lecture or discussion facilitates the acquisition of knowledge rather than skill. These tapes may be used to introduce you to a new subject or to consolidate what you have learned from other sources. You may well want to make notes on key points, so have a notebook handy and use them on public transport rather than car journeys.

# 6

# Computer-based Learning

Computer-based learning (CBL) is a generic term which includes all methods of using computers in support of learning. An alternative description is technology-based training (TBT).

A number of video-based training programmes are now available on CD-i (compact disc interactive), enabling you to participate in interactive exercises that have been added to the original scripts.

The technology is developing so quickly that almost anything written on this subject will be immediately obsolete. So, to keep up to date, read IT (information technology) magazines, training magazines and use a learning resource centre.

The general advantages of CBL are:

- you can use the material at a time of your choosing
- if it is truly interactive it will enable you to learn at your own pace, with as much trial and error as you wish
- it can record the pattern of your learning, to help you analyse your strengths and weaknesses
- a well-designed program can be fun to use.

The main disadvantage is the cost of designing a tailor-made package. Economies of scale feature strongly: if you are the training manager of a multi-branch company, such as a travel agency or a chain of off-licences, these high start-up costs may soon be recouped. Equipment costs are, however falling all the time, and today's school-leavers take CBL for granted in a way which their parents continually struggle to catch up with.

# 7

# Study for a Professional Qualification

Every type of job, whether it is classified as a "profession" or not, has an institute, society or association representing its employees. A profession is defined as an occupation in a special area of activity, offering a distinctive service which is practised by people who have undertaken advanced training and education.

Normally there are various categories of membership, from student to experienced professionals. Membership can depend on passing examinations; or a person may qualify simply by length of experience; sometimes there are no entry criteria at all, other than an interest in the occupation.

Non-corporate members, such as students or graduates, are only partly qualified; corporate members are fully qualified by examination and experience. The level of examinations is of degree standard.

Methods of study towards these exams are broader than they used to be, and can include:

- open learning
- personal and postal instruction, combined with a period working with an experienced professional
- attending courses in colleges.

You obviously need to read through the specific procedures of your own institute. But a general point is that professional bodies are increasingly flexible over APL (accreditation of prior learning): through experience or by gaining an earlier, apparently unrelated, qualification, you may be exempt from some of the exams set by the institute. A good tutor can help you to build up a personal portfolio, which will demonstrate your ability and save you hours of unnecessary study.

# 8

# Undertake an Open Learning Programme

Defining open learning as learning "in your own time, pace and place" may not be original but is hard to improve upon.

Essentially, open learning involves working through a study programme in your own time, using guided reading (see No. 2), often backed up by videos. Good open learning material also includes methods for checking your understanding, such as self-assessment or tutor-marked tests, essays with feedback and work-based assignments.

The very advantage of open learning over traditional courses – namely that you can learn at home – also carries with it the problem of loneliness, and means that you need considerable willpower to persevere with your studies in the face of other attractions (or distractions). So open learning programmes often include periodic tutorials, either as a one-to-one meeting with your tutor or, more often, with a small group of fellow-students. Members of such a group will often ring each other up at intervals to ask for help, to give encouragement or just to have a chat.

A range of support mechanisms are on offer, including not only local study groups but computer conferencing, E-mail, residential workshops and a mentor (see No. 34).

How do you eat an elephant? In bite-sized chunks. An open learning programme such as an MBA degree can seem a huge undertaking. Therefore, it's a great help if you can break down the study into smaller stages and get feedback as you go along.

Three factors have combined to ensure the growth of open learning:

- new working patterns involving part-time and flexible hours
- rapid advances in computer technology
- imaginative design of materials to overcome "the loneliness of the long-distance learner".

# 9

# Gain an NVQ

A National Vocational Qualification (NVQ), and its Scottish equivalent (SVQ), is an award that recognises what you are capable of doing at work. You do not require formal qualifications to embark on gaining an NVQ, and there are no exams. Representatives of each occupational group, known as "lead bodies", have defined the standards of performance required in their sectors.

There are five levels of NVQ, starting with the performance of routine tasks and extending up to degree level. Performance is assessed at the workplace by a trained assessor, and the qualifications are awarded by institutions such as City and Guilds, BTEC and RSA.

Each NVQ is made up of a number of units, which you can work through one at a time. There are no age limits or time limits, and providing you can demonstrate the required ability you will gain the qualification. So it may not be necessary to attend any formal training course as such. It is up to you how you wish to learn: at work, at home or at a college or other training centre.

The detailed structure of NVQs and the assessment processes are quite complicated, but that is an issue of more concern to training managers than candidates. You can obtain guidance on your own way forward through your training manager, your Training and Enterprise Council (TEC) or your local college. Initially, the complexity of the system put many people off the idea. But there is now a clear sharpening of interest by individuals, keen either to strengthen their CVs or to gain encouragement in their personal growth.

The Management Charter Initiative (MCI) provides national programmes such as Crediting Competence, under which you produce a portfolio of evidence of your management ability which contributes towards an NVQ at level 3 or above.

As with professional qualifications (see No. 7), APL – accreditation of prior learning – is also a feature in the NVQ process. Any relevant experience gained from work, study, leisure or home life may contribute knowledge and skills towards an NVQ.

# 10

# Visit other Organisations

This method involves visiting with a group of people (visits carried out on your own are dealt with in Nos. 22 and 44).

Group visits can usefully be divided into two types. The first involves a visit to another organisation to hear a presentation or take part in a meeting (e.g. with fellow-members of your professional body, Chamber of Commerce, trade union, network group, etc). On this sort of visit you may only see a limited part of the host organisation's premises and meet a few of its staff. But even so, in addition to the intrinsic value of the presentation or meeting, you may also gain by making comparisons with your own organisation. Pay particular attention to their reception arrangements. The best firms go out of their way to gain feedback from visitors. TR Fastenings in Sussex, for example, invite all visitors to complete a simple one-page questionnaire which asks for suggestions about any aspect of the company. Another feature to watch for is notice boards, which in many organisations are not used to anything like their full effect. (Do all notices have an expiry date? Does every notice show the name of its originator? etc.)

The second type of visit is the tour, where you are shown round a significant part of the premises. If you are planning such a visit, ensure that there will be sufficient hosts to split your group into small numbers, as everyone must be able to hear and see clearly.

In any factory visit, noise levels can seriously impair the potential learning, so people must be able to cluster closely round their guide. Often the most valuable learning comes from talking to people at random during the tour: any organisation which shields you from this has something to hide. A group of civil servants visited the Premier Brands factory on Merseyside, and were continually waylaid by shop-floor workers thrusting Jaffa cakes at them – their pride and commitment was exhilarating.

Group visits must include an opportunity for debriefing. Although this may take place at the end of a tour over a cup of tea with the hosts, it can be rather superficial. So, arrange a private debriefing, limited to the members of your group, as soon as possible after the visit so that the learning points can be distilled.

# 11

# Action Learning

After a remarkably long period in which action learning failed to take root in the UK, it is now growing in popularity. In essence it is one of those simple and obvious ideas: a small group (usually 4–6 people), called a "set", come together at regular intervals and share their work problems and successes. In the early stages the set uses a facilitator, whose main role is to help them understand the learning process. This done, he/she should then gradually fade into the background, leaving the set to carry on under their own steam. The critical success factors for action learning are:

- confidentiality: participants discuss real people and unburden themselves to each other
- consistency: a set must meet at reasonably regular intervals (once every three weeks for half a day is common), and substitutes are not allowed

- sharing: participants must want to learn, not just chat, which requires a willingness to help each other on a mutual basis.

Action learning sets have been used within a single organisation (e.g. Surrey County Council has nearly 100 managers taking part) or with a mixed membership. One set in the west of England consisted on a head teacher, a vicar, a newspaper editor, a district nurse and a production manager. Some sets prefer to meet on neutral territory, off-site.

The very name "action-learning" says a great deal. The aim is not to set up a talking shop, but rather a platform for taking action, and the ultimate outcome is learning: what works, what doesn't; insights into stubborn problems; lateral thinking; drawing courage from colleagues.

# "Adopt" a Company

Staff in organisations such as executive agencies or newly privatised utilities find themselves on a steep learning curve when it comes to understanding the commercial marketplace. For them, and for anyone wanting to understand an organisation in the round, "adopting" a company is an innovative and fascinating experience.

The idea grew out of a number of self-managed learning groups for civil servants set up by The Industrial Society. Members of the group select a public company and "adopt" it over a period of months. They research it from every angle: gathering press cuttings; obtaining its annual report; buying product samples, if appropriate; talking to its customers and suppliers. They buy a few shares and monitor their progress on the stock market; and they attend the company's AGM. Once the picture is becoming clear, they contact the company and either ask if they may visit as a group, or invite one of the company's managers to visit them. They make a presentation to the company, pointing out its strengths and weaknesses and asking a lot of searching questions: in effect, adopting the approach of an independent auditor or consultant. Companies are very intrigued to be approached by intelligent outsiders in this way, and usually respond positively.

If you approach the "adoption" enthusiastically, it will help you to identify with the company and experience what it feels like. You will find yourself looking at issues in the round, as overall business issues rather than simply marketing or finance.

The same principle can be applied, with modifications, to "adopting" a charity, a school or a health authority.

# Serve on a Task Force or Working Party

Nowadays so much work gets done through project teams that one sometimes wonders if there is anyone left within departments as we know them! On the whole this is a totally healthy trend, as it breaks down the artificial barriers which so often bedevil organisations of any substantial size.

There is, of course, a huge variety of project teams, working parties and task forces. But they share a number of common characteristics:

■ They are set up for a limited period to tackle a defined issue.

- They draw on people from several departments, and quite often from several levels of seniority.
- They have authority from a senior level to draw on resources (money, information, time) when they are needed.
- They ultimately report back with recommendations and/or actions to whoever authorised their creation.

Some groups of this kind operate formally, with tight terms of reference. Some are much looser and spend more time in brainstorming mode. Quality circles often fall into the latter category, having a roving commission to come up with new answers to all problems. For example, they may focus on some acknowledged bottleneck in production, or any other process where faults often occur. By using the creativity of members of the group, assumptions are challenged, alternatives explored and improvements (very often simpler than the original method) implemented.

Such groups acquire distinctive names: in Reuters they are called SIGs (special interest groups); in Jardinerie Garden Centres they are PIGs (project initiation groups) which in turn breed Piglets, small teams tackling specific issues. Forty out of Jardinerie's 200 employees have taken part in such groups already.

Project teams can be excellent for developing your skills. You should be able to improve your problem-solving techniques (such as 80/20, SWOT, critical success factors, etc), your knowledge of other parts of the organisation and your time management. And you can also network with the other members of the team long after the project targets have been achieved.

# 14

# Participate in a Business Game or Simulation

A business game is played out between two or more teams. The same data is presented to each team: usually you and your colleagues role-play senior managers in a company which is competing in the marketplace against rival companies. Time is compressed so that ten minutes of real time represents perhaps one month of trading. At intervals you have to make decisions, which are fed into a computer. You are then given fresh data about your position *vis-à-vis* your competitors. Umpires for the business game can also inflict sudden surprises on your team, e.g. a strike or collapse of a supplier.

For most people the challenges in a business game, and thus the learning opportunities, lie in:

- having to play a role which may be totally new to you (e.g. a production manager in real life has to become a purchasing director in the game)
- the speed with which you have to make decisions (you are forced to work as a team because no one team member has all the relevant information)
- the need to be both proactive and reactive (although you may make splendid plans, your opponents are planning too, so you must learn to anticipate competitor activity and to respond to it rapidly once it becomes apparent).

To gain maximum value from a business game, there are two traps you should avoid. The first is to criticise the "unreality" ("In real life we would have more time", "In real life a company wouldn't make such a silly mistake", etc). The second is to worry unduly about numerical accuracy. Some people panic when asked to make rapid calculations; but as long as your figures are roughly right, that is sufficient. Winning teams in business games are those which spend as much time as possible on strategic decision-making, not on working everything out to four decimal places.

A good business game is exhausting fun, but it is also an expensive learning instrument and requires expert tutors. Finally, remember that a thorough debriefing period is essential if collective and individual learning is to be assimilated.

# 15 Self-managed Learning

With old-fashioned training you wait to be on the receiving end of training. Self-managed learning (SML) is the very opposite: you take on responsibility for your own learning.

This means that the agenda can be tailored to your needs, but it does not mean that you have to work alone. Working with colleagues in an SML group, facilitated in the early stages by a tutor, is usually the best method.

There are many varieties of SML programmes, but they often share these features:

■ The organisation draws up a "shopping list" of themes: e.g. marketing, managing change, Japanese management, etc.

- Participants work in groups of 6–10, and select a number of themes to pursue as a group.
- The group plans its own meetings, to be held at intervals over several months. These may include visits, guest speakers, a business game, etc.
- Each participant also tackles some themes individually: e.g. by guided reading, project work, workshadowing, etc.
- Individual learning should be shared with the group, so that all can benefit. A remarkable amount of learning can be achieved by listening to another's experiences and analysing them together.
- The group can be assisted in the early stages by a tutor, whose main role is to help the group learn how to learn. This might include questionnaires on learning styles, refresher sessions on sources of information, tips on rapid reading, etc. The tutor can also offer ideas, and counsel as required, but will have failed if he/she is still playing a strong part after several meetings. The best tutors gradually retreat into the background.

Self-managed learning can accommodate any subject you like, delivered by any method you like. Much of the pioneering work on adopting a company (see No. 12) and external project attachments (No. 22) was carried out as part of SML programmes.

The single most important ingredient in SML is planning. You need to consider timescale, resources, "shopping lists", evaluation and other issues. But if it is well planned, it can be the most stimulating learning experience you have ever undergone.

# 16

# Outdoors Training

The purpose of outdoors training is not usually to make you physically fit, although awareness of your fitness may be an outcome. Advocates of outdoors training use it for a variety of reasons:

- For an *individual*: to build confidence in his/her abilities; to strengthen self-awareness; to improve assertiveness; to improve interpersonal skills; to enhance leadership ability.
- For a *team*: to build teamwork; to recognise that different team members contribute in different ways; to improve planning; to respond effectively to crises; to break down barriers of status, age and gender.

There are many centres throughout the country which specialise in outdoors training. They tend to use a variety of natural settings: lakes, cliffs, moorland, etc, and often hostel-type, basic accommodation with self-catering; although some centres provide luxurious hotel-type accommodation as a contrast to the rigours of the outdoor exercises.

The more extreme examples deliberately subject participants to severe discomfort (e.g. having to swim across a cold lake to reach your breakfast), and generally push people near to their limits of endurance. At the other end of the spectrum are centres where the physical effort required for the exercises is slight and more attention is paid to planning skills than to stamina.

Activities can include canoeing, abseiling, cross-country expeditions (involving camping overnight), obstacle courses, rock-climbing, crossing a gorge on a rope, orienteering, etc.

Of course safety is paramount. Before using any outdoor centre you *must* satisfy yourself of their safety precautions and the capability of their tutors, and ensure that you are medically fit to tackle the exercises.

Consider carefully your objectives for using this form of training. You may well have several aims, including sheer curiosity and a wish to "try anything once". If you clarify these in your own mind, you are less likely to be disappointed.

Inevitably, of course, horror stories abound of sadistic ex-paratroopers screaming insults at participants on outdoor programmes. But there are some highly effective centres where learning and confidence come as much through encouragement by fellow-team members as from anything else. One of the key tasks of the tutors is to ensure a richly productive debriefing after each activity, and to produce a cumulative process of learning rather than a series of disjointed exercises.

You need to be ready for a "high" of immediate post-course euphoria followed by a "low" a few months later when the excitement has worn off. So, back at the workplace, it is especially important to reinforce what has been learned in the outdoors setting (see No. 38). If you have taken your team with you to the training, lead by example "back at the ranch" by putting your teamwork into practice. If you have attended the course on your own, discuss it in detail with your manager, both before and after.

*Example:*

John Herring, a Customer Account Manager of Dowty Aerospace Landing Gear Ltd, attended an 'Effective Leadership' course at Wernside Caving Centre in Cumbria. This involved a number of syndicate 'task and review' sessions, in which a leader and observer were nominated. These varied from ten minute tasks to whole-day exercises.

His comment was: 'This method gave an opportunity to try new and different leadership styles in addition to my usual style, and receive very blunt and honest appraisals from a peer-group.

However, the leadership of a peer-group can be artificial in that motivational issues are not so important with a group of managers. Stopping other team members from taking over can be a side-distraction.

I learnt a great deal about my style and actions, where both leading and following were perceived by others. The outdoors training was also useful practice in rapid-planning and observation skills'.

# 17

# Attend a Training Course

It is often the case that an alarming proportion of people who attend external training courses have been sent as a reward or as a punishment. Neither of these is a valid motive. Moreover, to have been "sent" implies that the course participant is passive, waiting for things to happen rather than taking any control over his/her own development. To avoid this behaviour, have a thorough discussion with your manager before attending any training course whether internal or external, but especially external. This briefing should include:

■ the course objectives, and whether these concern knowledge, skills or behaviour, or a combination of all three
■ how achievement of these objectives can be measured and

what reinforcement of your learning will be supplied after the course, whether by your manager, colleagues or your own actions
- how your participation in the course should contribute to the objectives of the organisation as well as being of value to you personally
- any clarification or reassurance you may need about the style of the course and how demanding you may find it.

You may question the need for such in-depth briefing, but it is The Industrial Society's experience that course members sometimes arrive nervous, apprehensive and inadequately briefed. Some of the tutor's energy then has to go towards relaxing them before they can begin to benefit from the course content. Much of this is avoidable.

Whatever topic the course covers, only part of the event's potential value lies in its content: the hidden benefit comes from what you learn from the other course members. If you attend an internal course and meet colleagues from other parts of your organisation, do not miss the opportunity to get to know them better. Your subsequent contact with them will be enhanced. If the course is external, you have a (literally) once-in-a-lifetime chance to network with a range of other organisations.

You can obtain invaluable feedback on how your own organisation looks to outsiders by talking to them – sometimes you will feel proud, sometimes chastened. And it's a good idea to select two or three people and keep in touch with them for months afterwards; all sorts of commercial leads open up in this way, and all sorts of informal benchmarking can result.

To help you select an appropriate external course you can use TAPS or the National Training Index (see Resources section).

# Undertake a Secondment to Another Organisation

Secondments come in all shapes and sizes, but in this context we can take a secondment to mean a period of at least a month – sometimes as long as two or three years – where you transfer to another organisation and become part of it, reporting to a manager in the host organisation; but returning afterwards to your own employer.

In some cases the main purpose is to make a contribution to

the community; in others it is primarily for your own development. A number of well-trodden routes now exist: between industry and government departments, reciprocally; between industry and education, reciprocally; and from companies to the voluntary sector. A very useful report on secondments by the Centre for Employment Initiatives highlights a range of management benefits that can result from mid-career secondments. Among these are:

- enhancing skills and experience ("It was an opportunity to test out if he would be able to make the change from engineering to management and administration")
- clarifying the future or having a break ("Secondment offered change without risk – she was in a rut and her skills were not being used by the company")
- filling a gap ("He needed to move on, but no job was available; we needed time, otherwise he would have had to leave the company").

Whatever the motives, every secondment needs very careful planning; not just on your part but also by the host organisation. The planning should include the following: an induction programme; a nominated sponsor; arrangements to keep you informed about your own organisation while you are away; and a re-entry programme. Some useful publications are listed in the Resources section.

A well-planned secondment can bring great benefits to the individual, his/her own employer and the host organisation. A good example was the case of Sue Winter, motoring buyer for B&Q, who was seconded for two years to the Prince's Youth Business Trust. Eventually becoming a regional manager for the Trust, she had nothing but praise for the concept. "This secondment has vastly widened my overall perception of business". B&Q's marketing director described it as "a brilliant opportunity" and the Trust were delighted as well. And NatWest Bank has recently started seconding some of its branch managers to work in small companies for six weeks, so that they can experience at first-hand the the reality of life in the small business.

# Take up Office in the Community

Devoting some of your "free" time to develop skills relevant to work is an option which will obviously be determined by your domestic circumstances as well as by your own willpower. Many people who throw themselves enthusiastically into voluntary activities do not manage to transfer the skills which they develop there into the workplace.

The accompanying diagram illustrates the possibilities that are available. The four quadrants represent opportunities for learning. Planned learning within the job could be through being coached; planned learning away from the job, for a florist, for example, might come from strolling through the local parks, picking up ideas for floral displays. Unplanned learning within the job might come through discussing with a colleague why a product launch had failed or succeeded. Unplanned learning away from the job could happen by realising that a method you had used to chair a meeting of your Neighbourhood Watch group could work just as well in your office.

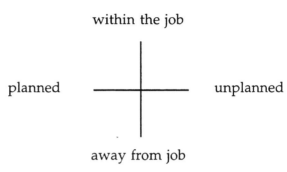

within the job

planned ———————— unplanned

away from job

Finding opportunities will depend on your personal interests. Obviously, they will be more readily available if you take office as chair, treasurer, secretary, stage manager or something similar: arguably it requires greater skill to achieve a concerted approach in a voluntary organisation, with no sanctions, than in paid employment. The histrionics on stage in the amateur dramatic society are nothing compared to those backstage!

To help you transfer your learning, you may find it useful to have a mentor (see No. 34). Common lessons that can be learned in voluntary work include the importance of consulting people, the need to stick to agreed objectives, project management and listening skills.

# 20

# Undertake a Secondment or "Job-swap" within your Organisation

In many large organisations people often have only a fleeting impression of other parts of their company. When you get the chance to see for yourself – even if it's only a half-day visit – your opinion may change considerably. And more often than not this change is for the better, because you meet people in the flesh and begin to appreciate the constraints under which they are working.

Organisations where considerable energy is apparently spent

outflanking other departments would therefore do well to consider using job-swaps or short internal secondments. British Steel, for instance, arranged for several managers of their Welsh plants to swap jobs for three months – a salutary experience all round.

An obvious opportunity for an internal secondment is covering for a colleague who is absent on maternity leave.

With "delayering" and flatter structures, conventional "vertical" promotion opportunities are becoming much rarer. So internal secondments should start to grow significantly. Your chances of achieving promotion will be dramatically enhanced if you can show firsthand experience of several functions in the organisation, rather than intensive experience in only one. In future, a typical career pattern will consist of a central function which is your natural home – whether finance, human resources, marketing, etc – to which you keep returning from a series of short excursions (secondments) to other parts of the organisation.

# 21

# Undertake a Sabbatical

The sabbatical system developed in universities. After several years in a post, a lecturer would be encouraged to take anything from a term to a year off to teach in another institution, conduct research abroad or in some other way refresh his/her mind and spirit.

Some companies award sabbaticals, including Post Office Counters, Prudential and the John Lewis Partnership. A sabbatical is not the same as a secondment (see No. 18); it is designed to meet your personal, unique needs and circumstances, and does not necessarily involve being based in any organisation. For example:

- George S. took a six-month sabbatical from his teaching post to write a book at a cottage in the Lake District.

- Jean H. took a three-year unpaid career break to bring up her children. She returned to work for three weeks each year and was sent regular bulletins about her organisation. During this period she also undertook guided reading (see No. 2). After her career break she was reinstated at her previous job grade, but in a different post.
- Philip B. took a nine-month sabbatical, which included an extended tour in the Pacific (part business, part holiday) to enhance his knowledge of marine biology.

There are all manner of qualifying periods for sabbaticals. But for our present purpose we should concentrate on the development benefits:

- Refreshment and renewal. A normal holiday provides this to some extent. A sabbatical is longer, and because you take it at your own pace it should give you new zest on your return to work.
- A sense of perspective. In the same way as a religious retreat provides a calm haven for a jaded mind, a sabbatical should enable you to step outside your day-to-day working environment.
- Establishing new contacts with whom you can network well beyond the period of the sabbatical.

Because a sabbatical can be planned well ahead, it should provide the opportunity to involve your family to a greater extent than a secondment normally would.

# 22

# Carry out a Short Project Attachment to Another Organisation

This is a much-underused method which has considerable potential. As with "adopting" a company (see No. 12), part of the benefit comes from seeing an organisation through fresh eyes. The project attachment is your sole responsibility, but you may need the help of a tutor or mentor to identify a realistic project and a host organisation. The attachment works like this. You identify a subject area which you want to know more about – it could be anything from induction procedures to the layout of a department store. You then draw up a short-list of organisations within reasonable travelling distance where such a subject might be relevant. Through your tutor, or by using your networks (see No. 47), approach these organisations with a clearly defined project theme. Then, in discussion, refine the theme into one which will form a genuinely useful project which you can tackle in only a few working days.

To the host organisation this can be a very attractive proposal: an intelligent outsider looks at a real problem and recommends answers after only a few days. And there is no cost (except negligible time in clarifying the project objectives) to the host.

Before carrying out your project, you must do your homework. You will be faced with two simultaneous and steep learning curves: the subject-matter and the host organisation. So make sure you read up about both beforehand.

The host organisation will provide you with a guide or sponsor, who will show you around and make appointments in advance. But for the most part it is up to you. In one particular project, a civil servant investigated a bottleneck of mail that had built up at Brighton Post Office as a result of masses of circulars from financial services companies. In one week he was able to recommend a way of re-routing this mail through an underused branch office, so releasing the log jam.

In another example, a manager helped redesign literature for a tourist board; yet another reduced staff turnover in a brewery. The Industrial Society has facilitated 1,400 of these short, sharp project attachments all over the country. The typical length is five working days, with a further day to present a report and recommendations.

People react with great enthusiasm to these projects, which are both challenging and satisfying. But the benefits become particularly apparent when you report back to your own organisation: colleagues profit from learning about your experiences, and ways of applying the learning in your own environment emerge more readily.

*Example:*

A civil servant undertook a one week project attachment in a hotel. Her assignment was to review the hotel's development programme for chefs.

The hotel manager read the report which she wrote after her attachment and commented:

"This paper is immediately of great and real value to us, stating clearly and succinctly the strengths and weaknesses of the chef development programme. It is uncluttered with speculation and supposition: her observations and prescribed courses of action are sensible, objective and realistic.

Her success has been due to a number of factors:

- She is not a caterer and is therefore unbiased, she has no axe to grind.

- She is able to relate to people very quickly and gain their confidence.

- She unearths a lot of information in a short space of time."

# 23

# Workshadowing

Workshadowing is designed to offer an insight into the reality of another person's job. The objective is to bring the job to life, "warts and all", allowing you to experience it at very close quarters without having to carry the job out yourself or undergo any training. Sometimes workshadowing is carried out within your own organisation, sometimes externally.

Usually, a workshadowing attachment lasts a couple of days, or perhaps a week. Arrangements are made for you, the "shadow", to accompany a job holder throughout that whole period, sitting in as a silent observer while he/she takes telephone calls, attends meetings, visits suppliers, interviews staff, drafts reports, etc.

At convenient points the job holder discusses with you the activity he/she has just completed and answers your questions. Your aim is to find out *what* he/she does and *why*.

Often, but not always, the job holder is senior to you, and may be involved in confidential discussions, so there might be short periods when you are not allowed to be present; but with good planning this can be minimised.

Workshadowing can be very valuable in career planning, because it gives you an insight into the challenges and frustrations of a particular job in a way which a job description or advertisement may not convey. You can then decide whether you want to aim towards this post, either for promotion or as a sideways move.

Careful briefing is essential. The job holder needs to understand your objectives in advance; if at all possible the two of you should meet beforehand. The job holder's immediate staff and colleagues, together with anyone he/she is scheduled to meet during the shadowing period, must be informed in advance that you will be there. Debriefing after the shadowing period is also important; this can take place with your own manager or with a trainer or personnel officer.

Shadowing has proved popular with a wide range of people, from graduate trainees and students at school, to administrative staff, middle managers and technical specialists.

# 24

# Act as a Non-executive Director

Although a non-executive director has no day-to-day responsibilities within the organisation and does not manage any of its staff, he/she is fully accountable in law as a director.

Often non-executives are given special responsibilities, such as serving on an audit committee or on a remuneration committee which sets the salaries of the executive members of the board.

In recent years the increased attention paid to corporate governance means that the position of non-executive director is no sinecure. By the same token, it does offer an unrivalled method of developing your managerial skills. The ideal sequence is to become a non-executive director of another organisation before being promoted to the post of an executive director in your own. In this way, you serve a kind of apprenticeship before becoming a fully fledged director.

The great value of non-executive directors to the organisation is their independence; they are neither jousting for promotion nor representing any particular function within the business. From your point of view this independence provides a great opportunity. For example, if your own career has been mainly based in marketing, as a non-executive director you will need to look at issues in a broader context because marketing is probably represented already on the board through an executive director. You are free to ask the "idiot questions" – those questions which are often so obvious that no one has asked them before, but which get to the root of the matter. You will also have to extend your time frame: being a non-executive director is much more about planning the future than organising the present.

The range of organisations that require non-executive directors is now very wide, and includes housing associations, hospital trusts, charities and schools, as well as companies. A matching service is provided by Pro Ned (Promotion of Non-Executive Directors), whose address is given in the Resources section.

# 25

# Deputise for your Manager

By "deputise" we meaning having full authority to act in your manager's absence. If your manager has a clash of diary engagements and you have to attend a meeting in his/her place, you are not genuinely deputising if you say little at the meeting, make notes and relay them back to your manager afterwards. In that situation you would merely be a messenger, not a deputy.

A genuine deputy has the authority to act, in effect, as the temporary manager, and to take decisions which carry just as much weight. Contrast these two scenarios:

1 Your manager is suddenly taken ill and is absent from work for ten days. No one could have foreseen this, and

your ability to deputise is bound to be constrained as you will not have had time to study his/her current workload in detail in advance. So you may have to refer some decisions upwards to your M2 (ie. the manager two levels up from you).

2  Your manager plans to take two weeks holiday two months ahead. Here you have ample time to become a genuine deputy. Some weeks ahead, you should discuss together your strengths and weaknesses in relation to the manager's role. Improve your weak areas (they may only be "weak" in the sense of lack of experience, rather than lack of competence) through a relevant method, e.g. coaching supplemented by reading.

A few days before your manager's holiday, you must do two things. First, your manager should let his/her colleagues know that you will be deputising, and that you have full authority. This must also be understood by all his/her direct reports. Second, you and your manager should go through the diary for the whole fortnight to ensure that you are fully prepared for meetings, correspondence, visits or whatever else is due to take place.

During your manager's absence you may find it very helpful to keep a daily learning log (see No. 4). This will inform the debriefing discussion on your manager's return.

While you are deputising, you do not have to be the world's expert on every subject. Managers who take every decision alone, never "thinking aloud" with a colleague or consulting their team, are not good managers. Asking for suggestions, or seeking guidance, simply enriches the quality of the decision; it does not absolve you from accountability for it.

Some status-conscious managers find it difficult to delegate sufficiently to allow you to act as a real deputy. If your manager is like this, it may help to separate his/her role into its two aspects: the added value of the post and the added value contributed by the manager as an individual (his/her unique experience, talents, personal style, etc). By definition, you cannot emulate the second aspect (although you can bring your own added value instead). But you should be allowed to carry out the first.

## 26

# Take on New Responsibilities

When successful senior managers are asked to look back over their careers, they will quite often say that one of their most formative experiences was having to take on a new responsibility at short notice. It may have been caused by some emergency, such as reorganising after a major fire, or by the sudden illness of a colleague. Whatever the reason, what stretched them was the suddenness, the challenge of coping with the unplanned event.

If your natural learning style is that of "activist" (see No. 36), you will relish the challenge. If you are naturally more cautious, you may start rationalising all sorts of excuses: I'm not prepared; the risk is too great; we may upset the customers, etc. It may help to remember that progress depends on our willingness to take risks: the space age could not have come about without the bravery of pioneer astronauts.

In the worst sort of "political", status-ridden organisations, your colleagues will want you to fail (which may only spur you to make a go of it in spite of them). But in any halfway-civilised organisation, colleagues will want you to succeed in your new responsibilities. This will certainly be the case with your own team members, whose job satisfaction derives from being on a winning rather than a losing team.

Two other elements can help. Firstly, if you have a mentor (see No. 34), this is when he/she can be of great help, by making sure you concentrate on key issues, and don't get sidetracked, and reminding you of your strengths. Secondly, "little and often" entries in your personal learning log (see No. 4) will enable you to see our progress and problems in perspective. Problems don't go away, but if you re-read your log at intervals, it should reveal how a task which proved difficult a month ago appears much less daunting now.

# 27

# Represent your Organisation or Profession

In this situation your main responsibility is to act as a valid representative. Your "constituency" might be your company, e.g. if the trade association for your industry sector sets up an advisory committee on technical matters. The association's own technical experts make the final decisions but value the views of a cross-section of companies. Make it widely known within your company that you are performing this role, and ensure that you are well briefed, so that you can put over your company's view confidently.

Alternatively, your "constituency" may be your profession,

as distinct from your employer. This is a more taxing role, because you have more work to do in canvassing the views of your peers in the profession. The committee might be a joint one representing several professions, and your task would be to ensure that your colleagues are well represented in the debates. You may have to send out questionnaires, visit colleagues in other locations and play an active part in branch meetings in order adequately to assess the views of your "constituents".

Either way, the responsibility can be time-consuming. To ensure that it does not become a chore, focus on the two main developmental opportunities it can provide:

1 It should hone your skills at marshalling, summarising and presenting data in a persuasive manner.
2 The way the advisory body runs its meetings should be instructive. Study the person in the chair; observe the politics involved in the sparring that goes on between different interest groups; select some of the contacts you make and network with them.

To be truly representative of your "constituents" you have to ensure that you convey their views clearly. Sometimes you may not personally agree with them, and it will normally be within your terms of reference to express your own opinion as well. In fairness to the people you represent, you should go out of your way to make clear the occasions when your view does not concur with that of the majority.

# 28

# Serve as a Staff Representative or Shop Steward

Trade unions and staff associations are set up with a small number of paid officials (national officers, etc) and a larger number of members who stand for election to represent the interests of their colleagues in the workplace.

The way in which staff representatives operate varies widely from one business sector to another, but generally they have four main roles:

1 To be consulted by managers over personnel policies and business plans.
2 To negotiate pay and conditions for their members.

3 To take up any grievances, or accompany members at disciplinary hearings.
4 To act as a communications link with the union's full-time officers.

The staff representative's role is not always easy, and can be stressful. But it provides an excellent training ground in influencing and negotiating skills, public speaking and committee work, and in understanding the commercial aspects of a business.

If you are interested in becoming a staff representative, you are unlikely to have many competitors for the post! Many employees see it as a thankless task and indeed it is not for the faint-hearted. But it can be very satisfying and progressive managements treat staff representatives with dignity, taking them into their confidence over sensitive issues.

To avoid misunderstandings over your role and responsibilities as a shop steward, you should make sure that on appointment you are issued with credentials that have been agreed between the employer and the trade union. Most unions also run short training courses to help staff representatives carry out their functions properly; sometimes such training is organised jointly by management and union.

# 29

# Serve an Education/Industry Link Organisation

Being a school governor belongs in No. 24, as a form of non-executive directorship, because a school governor is appointed as an individual, not as a representative of his/her company. But there are many other ways in which you can facilitate the interface between education and industry on behalf of your employer. The most obvious is to join an EBP (education/business partnership).

1994 figures show that 56% of primary and 92% of secondary schools now have some form of link with businesses and there is no shortage of initiatives at both national and local level. For example:

- Young Enterprise – school students set up miniature companies, marketing and selling real products. They need managers to act as advisers.
- Challenge of Industry conferences – The Industrial Society runs conferences in schools for sixth-formers, discussing real issues about managing people. Managers are needed as speakers and group advisers.
- Mentors – there is a national network of adult mentors for students at school.
- SATROs (Science and Technology Regional Organisations) – these organisations run events to stimulate children's interest in science. As an example, 44 primary-school students on Merseyside worked in teams to design and build a model car which would carry a small load and negotiate a bridge. The EBP manager commented that they created "a range of weird and wonderful vehicles, but most importantly it proved that science can be fun".

Business in the Community co-ordinates many of these education/industry initiatives, and publishes regular newsletters. One of your main learning opportunities in this field is to design events which involve young people in a hands-on capacity and not merely as passive listeners.

## 30

# Work on a Community Project

Community projects merit a separate entry from education/industry links (see No. 29) because there are so many of them to choose from.

Some companies might adopt a particular charity for a five-year period, whereas others may choose a different one each year. If you work for such a company, you have the chance to join a team of colleagues working on a project for the chosen charity.

A number of companies organise internal competitions to promote this sort of work, e.g. Halifax, the financial services company. They encourage all their staff to enter a selection process to join regional teams called Community Development Circles.

Other employers go for the "big bang" approach, concentrating their efforts in one major fund-raising drive, such as a fête or gala day. These occasions provide plenty of scope for practising communication skills, influencing, persuading and listening.

Publications by the Charities Aid Foundation, the National Council for Voluntary Organisations and Business in the Community list many ways in which the voluntary sector benefits from help.

Whether you can arrange some time off for voluntary work, e.g. through a secondment or a project, or whether you undertake it in your own time, the possibilities are limited only by your imagination. Apart from the satisfaction of helping with a worthwhile cause, you can learn much about improvisation, resilience, perseverance and teamwork from the voluntary sector.

## 31

# Respond to Guidance from your Immediate Manager

Luck obviously plays a part in arranging whether you work for a manager who is naturally good at delegating and helping staff to blossom, or a status-conscious bully. Whether luck is on your side or not, you can learn much from your manager or even, at worst, how *not* to manage!

Too many managers still pay lip-service to the development of their staff, or hold people back because they are too valuable in their present roles to lose through promotion or transfer. If your manager is like this, consider which of the 50 methods in this book you can use to compensate for the lack of development you are receiving from him/her. In particular, consider whether a mentor (see No. 34) might provide a useful counterweight.

One of the most effective drills for working well with your manager is to have one-to-one discussions with him/her at regular intervals, fixing the dates in your diaries well ahead. By a one-to-one I mean a private discussion of half an hour or more, in which you review your priorities over the last month or two and agree new targets for the future.

Try to incorporate into these one-to-ones a discussion of your development needs. If you have an unenlightened manager, he/she is more likely to be receptive to this if you:

- take the initiative, and show your commitment to develop yourself rather than want to be trained (see No. 15)
- use the "carousel of development" (see No. 38) to anchor personal development to the needs of the organisation.

I would emphasise two other points that will help you get the most from your manager:

1 If you are aware of your own learning style (see No. 36) and that of your manager you can anticipate how he/she will coach you.
2 By becoming a skilled coach and delegator yourself (see Nos. 49 and 50) you will find it easier to exploit the coaching or delegation offered to you by your manager.

# 32

# Accept Newly-Delegated Responsibility

If you have carried out a piece of work ten times, it probably seems simple, but try to recall the first time you had to do it – it may well have felt daunting. So delegation is a very fruitful source of development.

The initiative to delegate a task to you may come from you or your manager. In either case, you need to be clear just how much scope you are being allowed. If the task has to be carried out in a specific way, then clearly there is very little scope for creativity; nevertheless, you may learn quite a lot just from the novelty of it. For example, you may realise that while the task itself is straightforward, its sensitive context might require that you inform or consult a number of other people in the course of carrying it out.

A greater opportunity for learning comes if you are free to discharge the task in a variety of ways. In this case, what is delegated to you is responsibility for outcomes rather than inputs – as long as you reach the desired destination, there are several possible routes. If your manager is a good developer of staff, he/she will realise that your approach to the task may be different – possibly even better. So try to negotiate some scope for this.

Remember a person who is reluctant to delegate is hampering his/her own growth.

For delegation to have any developmental value, it must stretch you. So if you feel a little apprehensive about taking on a delegated task, this probably means that it is just right for you. Obviously if you feel completely out of your depth, then it is beyond your reach, but a frisson of concern gets the adrenaline flowing and provides the right degree of challenge.

# 33

# Respond to All Round Feedback

Traditional appraisal schemes involved a dialogue between yourself and your immediate manager, with some additional brief comments by the manager two levels up.

Today, however, a very rapid shift is under way towards all round feedback. There are many versions, but essentially the purpose is to open up constructive comment from all sources within the organisation who have significant contact with you. This can include your own staff, colleagues in other departments and others at your manager's level. Some organisations go beyond this and draw not only on these internal sources but external ones, such as customers, suppliers, auditors, etc.

In most cases this rounded feedback is supplied once a year.

It may be filtered through anonymous questionnaires and facilitators, or it may come "straight from the shoulder". Some organisations arrange for the feedback to be provided more frequently.

An additional source of information may be provided by staff attitude surveys. These are also on the increase, and in many instances the survey will include measurements of satisfaction with each staff manager in areas such as ability to communicate, to inspire, to coach, to listen, and so on.

So far the signs are that these data are being provided in a very sensible and constructive frame of mind. Staff are delighted to be trusted to use the system in a responsible fashion.

If you have the opportunity to receive feedback in any of the above ways, seize it. Your impact on others is an absolutely vital feature in your personal development, and whatever emerges should be acted on. For example, most of us think we are good listeners, but if people don't perceive us as such we have to do something about it.

# 34

# Use Guidance from a Mentor

Mentoring is a confidential, one-to-one relationship in which you use a more experienced (usually more senior) person as a sounding-board and for guidance. The relationship may last for many months, even years, and much of the contact is intermittent. It is a protected, non-judgemental relationship which facilitates your development.

Your mentor is not normally your line manager, because part of the mentor's role is to act as a safety-valve for your feelings, and sometimes those will concern the way you are being managed.

Mentoring has traditionally been used for people in their first job, but in recent years the practice has rapidly grown at more senior levels. There is nothing whatever to feel ashamed about in using a mentor, even (or especially) if you are a very senior person yourself.

An internal mentor can be particularly helpful in guiding you through office politics and advising you what is worth worrying about and what can be left to evaporate. An external mentor will draw on experience in other organisations.

The worst way to use a mentor is to expect him/her to give you unfair advantages, for example by influencing the result of a promotion board. Quite apart from the illegality of such an action (because of equal opportunities legislation), any advantage gained would be very short-lived. The mentor's role is rather to help you gain a sense of perspective. Sometimes this will be achieved by jolting you out of staleness; sometimes by cheering you up; sometimes simply by letting you get things off your chest or listening while you think aloud.

Mentoring is not exactly the same as coaching (see Nos. 31 and 49), although a mentor will employ coaching skills from time to time. For one thing, mentoring must be one-to-one and private, while a coach can simultaneously and publicly work with half a dozen people or more.

# 35

# Identify a Manager who is Excellent at Developing People

This method is one of the most neglected, among our list of 50. This is not because we lack good people-developers; it has more to do with short-term pressures for current high performance, sometimes at the expense of people's longer-term growth.

The manager you are seeking is one of two types:

1 There are some people who are just instinctively good managers of staff. They often seem slightly taken aback at being regarded as such, because it all seems so natural and obvious to them.

2 There are other managers who are not necessarily "natural" managers but who tackle human resource development very conscientiously and regard it as their duty.

Either way, such a manager is a real gift to your development.

You may have to use your powers of persuasion to be transferred to your chosen manager's team, particularly if that part of the organisation is not an obvious stop on your career path. So the best approach may be a secondment (see No. 20) rather than a long-term move.

When successful, mature people are asked to look back on their development they often single out a particular manager as crucially important. And the comments they make have remarkable consistency:

"He/she . . .

- stretched me, was demanding to work for and didn't let me coast along
- gave me plenty of feedback – "little and often"
- helped me think things through for myself, by asking me lots of questions but without providing many answers
- made time for me even when busy
- encouraged me through difficult patches
- prompted me to use many different methods for my development
- had no favourites, and was tough but fair
- set high standards, but exemplified them."

This managerial profile can be summed up in the phrase "tough love". Another version of it was advocated by the late Mia Kellmer Pringle, who for years directed the National Children's Bureau. She listed four prerequisites for the healthy development of young people:

- Love
- Responsibility
- Praise and recognition
- Stimulating new experiences.

We may not require managers to love their staff, but we certainly need them to care about them as individuals. So with that slight amendment, the Pringle list will serve as well in this context.

If you are fortunate enough to manoeuvre yourself into working for a really good manager, you will never forgive yourself if you do not keep notes *at the time* of what you are learning from the experience (see learning logs, No. 4). Make the most of your one-to-one discussions (see No. 31), but also think through for yourself how much of the manager's effectiveness is due to his/her personality (which may be hard for you to emulate) and how much due to actions (such as the approach in *"The One-minute Manager"* – short, sharp feedback on the spot).

# 36

# Use Diagnostic Instruments

A minor industry has grown up in the last few years around questionnaires, tests and exercises, claiming to guide you in everything from choice of a career to which role to play in a team.

Among the dross there are several genuine and valuable instruments. One is the learning-styles questionnaire developed by Peter Honey (see Resources section). By answering 80 questions about your personal preferences, you can identify your natural style of learning as a combination from four, which he calls activist, pragmatist, theorist and reflector. This will help you to choose appropriate methods to help your learning, and also to strengthen your ability in the styles which come less easily to you. If you are in charge of other people (see No. 49), it will also enhance your coaching effectiveness.

There are several instruments available for diagnosing team roles. The three best-known examples are Belbin, the Margerison-McCann team management index and the Strength Deployment Inventory. Although their prime purpose is to aid the composition of teams, they each provide important insights for your own personal development. For example, they reveal how your natural team role can shift under pressure.

Other diagnostic instruments should only be used with the help of a qualified occupational psychologist or other person specially trained in their application. These instruments include critical thinking, spatial relationships, etc. You need to distinguish between tests which have right and wrong answers, such as intelligence tests, and inventories which simply show the kind of person you are.

For all types of diagnostic instrument, you must obtain thorough debriefing and feedback, to enable you to see the results in context and to use them to help your personal growth.

# 37

# Carry out a Constructive "Post-Mortem" on a Success or Failure

The purpose of a real post-mortem is to accept that a situation has happened, coolly examine the evidence, and then learn from it. In the same way, there are countless opportunities for post-mortems in the work context. It is important to separate any emotional overtones such as disappointment or elation: they are natural and need to be expressed, but try not to let them interfere with your assessment of what actually took place.

Suppose a big sales order has gone to a competitor. A thorough analysis should be undertaken to reveal trends. Factors could include speed of response, price, delivery dates, packaging, etc. You may discover learning points for the whole of your team or just for yourself.

Or, to cite a different example, suppose you revised the arrangements for your annual stocktaking, and succeeded in reducing by half the time taken by the previous system. This represents real success, and is worth examining. We tend to dwell over-much on failures instead of analysing success. So, ask yourself why did the new system go so smoothly? What were the crucial changes? Can we apply these principles to other parts of the business? Can we recognise the team's achievement in some way?

A post-mortem very soon after the event can be very motivating. At the BBC World Service, as soon as a broadcast is over the whole team will gather round and listen to a recording of the programme, discussing what went well and which areas need improving. Members of the team working together help to maintain the highest standards.

A post-mortem should not be a witch-hunt. Unless someone has been seriously negligent, there is no value in harping on failure. In a true learning organisation, a "have a go" climate will be actively promoted, and mistakes can be a positive source of learning. The key is to define parameters within which experiment is encouraged.

If you intend to use the post-mortem technique regularly, it may be helpful to develop a checklist of questions. By asking similar questions each time, clear trends will emerge. Also, by compiling the checklist in advance, you have done the cool analytical work ahead of the event, which makes it easier to achieve objectivity.

# 38

# Use the "Carousel of Development"

The accompanying diagram has evolved from several years of experience in the evaluation of training. In particular, it emphasises the need to establish the evaluation structure before training takes place rather than relegating it to an afterthought, as so often happens. You can make good use of it to plan your personal development; it forms a type of learning contract. And it only requires slight modification if you are a student or unemployed.

It is called a carousel because you go round each stage in the diagram and then repeat the process. Stages 1 and 6 are of most interest to top management in the organisation; stages 2 and 5 mainly concern yourself and your immediate manager together; and stages 3 and 4 are primarily the responsibility of the trainer, if a trainer is involved.

Stage 1 requires identification of a business need, to ensure that you are not undertaking development in a direction which will clash with the business. (If you are embarking on purely personal development, the business needs will not count, but make sure that you have consciously thought this through rather than casually overlooking it.) For example, if you want to learn Spanish but your employer does no business with Spain, you may nonetheless decide to carry on.

Stage 2 merits very careful consideration. If you define clear objectives for your development, your efforts will be repaid. These objectives need to be SMART (specific, measurable, achievable, realistic and time-bound). For example, if you feel that you are becoming stale in your work and desire a change of duties, what do you want such a change to achieve? Over what period? How will you measure the results? A dialogue with your manager, using your written draft of objectives, will prove invaluable here.

The outcome of the objective setting at Stage 2 will lead you directly to Stage 3, the choice of development method. You can narrow down which of methods in Section C would best meet the criteria you have just set. Let us suppose you decide on No. 22, a short external project attachment: you work out the details and then – Stage 4 – experience the process.

Now comes the test, in Stage 5. After your developmental experience, can you apply what you have learned in your own organisation? And can your immediate manager help reinforce your learning? Has the secondment delivered the SMART objectives which you and your manager agreed for it back at Stage 2?

Finally, at Stage 6, if your development was intended to contribute to the organisation as well as to you as an individual, has it done so? The evidence for this final stage may have a long gestation period – perhaps months or even years. Meanwhile other business needs will have emerged, so you can continue around the carousal to Stage 1 and start again with a new development process.

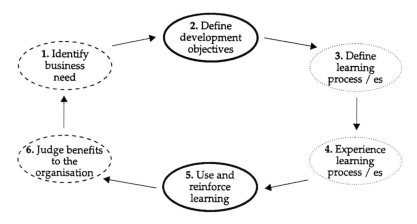

The Carousel of Development is copyright The Industrial Society

# 39

# Change the Way you Tackle your Work

We all acquire habits of tackling our work. Often these are effective: trial and error or years of experience may have proved that a particular method is best, or comes most naturally to you. But is easy for these habits to become stale, or for you to become unconsciously ineffective. Taking a critical look at work habits will keep you fresh and effective.

One useful check is activity sampling, a long-established technique in work study. Ask a colleague to note down, at intervals, what you are actually doing under appropriate headings, e.g. "talking on telephone", "writing a report", "searching in files", etc. (This needs to be properly planned – there are books available which contain random sampling tables, etc.) What the results reveal about your actual productivity can often be horrifying.

Another method is to ask someone to "shadow" you (see No. 23). This has a dual purpose: it allows your colleague to learn from your strengths, but it also enables them to draw your attention to wasted time, unnecessary repetition, etc.

A further method is process mapping, where you consider a task which you regularly carry out and split it into small sub-tasks, with the aim of streamlining, simplifying, combining or eliminating them. There are numerous time management aids on the market: diaries, planning charts, bring forward systems, etc.

A different starting-point is to challenge assumptions or to indulge in lateral thinking. For example, consider a regular task which you carry out alone. Does it have to be done alone? Would two brains be better than one? Similarly, do you have to be at your workplace every day? Could you be more productive by spending one day a fortnight working at home? Obviously, it depends on the nature of your work. Often, talking these issues through with a colleague will prove more fruitful than tackling them alone – you may be too close to the detail to see scope for change.

In the context of learning, the purpose of using any of the techniques described above is less about your efficiency (although that may improve) and more about the insights you will gain into your thought processes. Your ingrained methods of working may be blocking your creativity. The fiercest test of all is regularly to ask yourself: "What is my added value to the organisation, my unique contribution? What am

I best at? What can my particular mix of abilities and experience offer?" And having identified your added value, then assess how close you are to delivering it all of the time. The results will be salutary.

Another way of freshening up your working methods is to rewrite your job description. It should summarise the *outcomes* expected from your work, whereas many job descriptions concentrate on *inputs*. The more your job description specifies in detail what you are to do, the less scope you have for using your initiative, improving methods, and even questioning whether that task needs to be carried out at all. Some tasks must be tightly prescribed, for example for safety reasons; but even they are worth checking at least annually, to ensure that you are not artificially cramping your style.

# 40

# Use each Inspection as a Learning Opportunity

Nowadays there is no shortage of external comment on how organisations should be run. New regulatory bodies have proliferated – everything from Ofsted in schools to Lautro in unit trusts. If an organisation gains an award such as Investors in People or ISO 9001, it will be re-inspected at intervals.

These inspections, together with regular financial audits and occasional consultants' reports, are directed at the organisation rather than at individual employees. But you may nonetheless be able to learn from them and use this learning to aid your personal development.

If you are leading a team of people, such reports may bring out pointers about your management ability. For example, financial auditors are quick to draw attention to situations where authority has been delegated without adequate controls. Inspectors may also make suggestions on how to improve the retrieval of information.

If you are not in charge of other employees, different lessons may be learned from such inspections. Much will depend on your manager's attitude: if you can gain access to the report (e.g. if it is discussed at a team meeting) it may prove helpful in two ways:

1 Use the report as a model for reports which you yourself have to produce (see No. 41).
2 Look at the scope of the audit: what were the auditors looking for? What did they see as significant? Did they work to specific criteria? How did they organise themselves? It is revealing to see what outsiders comment on: often these turn out to be aspects that may have become routine and obvious to you as an insider.

You may also be able to learn from the inspectors' style of operating. Talk to colleagues who were interviewed by them. Did they put people at ease or did they appear threatening? Was their style appropriate?

# Write a Major Report

There are countless books on the skills of report-writing. This is not the place for tips on *how* to write a report, but rather a chance to consider report-writing as a learning opportunity.

There is no intrinsic virtue in writing a long report: Bernard Shaw once apologised for writing a long letter 'because I haven't time to write you a short one'.

But a substantial investigation or project will merit a substantial report. Such a task will hone your skills in marshalling considerable data and presenting it clearly. In doing this, you will mainly be using the left side of your brain – the analytical, logical, dispassionate, orderly side. You may feel strongly about the subject-matter: perhaps it is something in which you have invested considerable time and energy, e.g. a progress report on an exciting project, or an investigation justifying large capital expenditure. If you write the report well, you will let the facts speak for themselves, reserving your proposals until the final chapter. At this point you can draw on the right side of your brain, employing justified emotion and even passion to clinch your case.

Report-writing should also help you to present issues from the standpoint of a general manager or a consultant, to distance yourself from the detail in order to see the big picture. In addition, a well-argued report like this may also provide a fillip to your career prospects.

Whether your proposals are accepted or not, you can gain further benefit by asking an experienced person to give you a critique of your report. This person does not have to be an expert in the subject – for example, it would be an appropriate task for a mentor (see No. 34).

# 42

# Analyse the Actions of Effective Leaders

Whether or not you are in a leadership role yourself, you can benefit by discovering what makes for effective leadership in any walk of life. There are plenty of biographies and articles available on well-known leaders; but there are also initiatives which you yourself can take.

Firstly, if you want to meet a nationally known leader personally, consider arranging a small event for charity. Invite the relevant leader to speak, and allow him/her to choose the charity. (Naturally the selected person may not agree to your invitation, but couching it in the context of their favourite charity markedly increases your chances of success). The session can take one of three forms:

1 a straightforward talk followed by questions

2 an interview (you need to find a skilled person to carry this out for you)

3 a panel of questioners.

Alternatively, you can feature two or three leaders at the same event.

Secondly, not all effective leaders are national figures, nor are they necessarily very senior – a middle manager, the organiser of a voluntary service or a youth club leader can all be remarkable personalities from whom we can learn. So why not form a learning group with a few colleagues (see No. 15), and simply invite such leaders to come and talk informally with your group about how they approach their work?

It is important to remember the words at the top of this page: "the *actions* of effective leaders". It is much more productive to study their actions than to compile a list of abstract qualities (integrity, enthusiasm, etc) which mean different things to different people.

If you work in a bank, you can still learn from a leader in a hospital. The field of activity is not critical. If you think carefully, many of the actions taken by effective leaders are transferable to any sector.

# 43

# Take Part in a Debate

Perhaps because we see so much confrontational political debating on television, debating societies are less popular than they once were. But debating as a skill has much to recommend it as a method of development.

A debate is a formal discussion governed by rules of procedure. These normally include time-limits for speeches, the handling of interruptions, points of order, and so on. Some of this sounds – and indeed is – rather artificial when compared with the informal (not to say chaotic) process of arguing over a drink in the pub. But the constraints which the rules of debate impose are themselves a learning opportunity. Learning how to make three key points in as many minutes; gaining confidence by handling interruptions courteously but not being drawn off your track; winning over a sceptical or hostile audience: these are all opportunities afforded by participating in debates.

Because there are few local debating societies, and even fewer run at the workplace, it may be best to arrange two or three debates as a trial run. You can make up your own rules, and the subjects for debate can be a mixture of work-related and other themes. Of particular benefit to your development is if you speak on the opposite side to your instinctive views – e.g. if you are against Sunday trading, try proposing the case in favour. As with writing summaries or book reviews (see No. 3), this sharpens your critical faculties.

*Example:*

One organisation which offers debating experience is the British Junior Chamber (BJC). The BJC run Competitions and Awards, with debates organised as a contest between two teams; the winner being the team judged to be the most persuasive in putting across their side of the argument. It is important to appreciate that debating is a team effort and teams consist of two, four, or five speakers.

BJC is an out of hours training and leadership development organisation which offers its members unrivalled opportunities to develop their skills, both as individuals and within teams. In addition to formal training, members are given the chance to practise their skills in managing and leading projects internally within the local Chamber and externally in the community at a local, regional, national and international level. Membership is open to young people (18–40). For further information contact BJC Head Office, Tel: 01788 572795 Fax: 01788 542091.

# 44

# **Benchmarking**

Benchmarking – comparing your own business performance and practices against others – has blossomed in recent years. And the process of compulsory competitive tendering in the public sector has given the technique a particular boost.

You can benchmark:

- internally, against other departments
- functionally, against similar organisations who are not necessarily competitors (e.g. building societies and travel agents both have many small branch offices)
- against direct competitors
- across your business sector
- against acknowledged "world class" organisations.

The aim is to identify those factors which make the difference between average and excellent performance. There are various techniques available to help you compare like with like, some of which are quite sophisticated. To gain maximum value you have to be ruthlessly honest.

The Industrial Society's popular series of reports, entitled *Managing Best Practice*, covering such subjects as self-managed teams, induction, employee communication and empowerment, provides readable benchmarking data on which you can build your own comparisons.

As with inspections or audits, (see No. 40) benchmarking surveys are mainly undertaken for the organisation's benefit. But a survey is also likely to reveal many action points for you personally. Look out both for "hard" data (the actual performance your organisation or department has achieved) and also "soft" data (perceptions, image and attitudes, etc). Shaunne Shaw, General Manager Resourcing for British Airways, commented, "It is these soft service issues which give competitive edge, require organisational culture change, are more difficult to achieve and nearly impossible to copy."

# 45

# Join a User Group

A user group is the name given to an informal association of people from different organisations who are all using similar equipment or systems.

The most obvious source of such groups is information technology (IT). Organisations using the same type of computer software form a user group that is independent of the software house and usually self-financing, with minimal overheads. They arrange regular meetings, often taking it in turn to act as hosts (which can have the kind of spin-off benefits described in No. 10). They may sometimes invite a representative of the software house to attend.

"Cynics might argue that software houses have encouraged user groups simply as a way of extending business, but experience has shown that the relationship between a user group and a software house can be truly symbiotic, with both parties receiving great value from the link". (Colin Richards-Carpenter, "The advantages of user groups", *Personnel Management* December 1992).

The potential learning from such a group is obvious. For instance, you could involve other members of the group in a constructive post-mortem on success or failure (see No. 37). Or why not stage a debate (No. 43) on the respective merits of two approaches to IT?

One large-scale IT group is the IT Trainers' Forum, with four regions, each run by a committee of members with secretarial and administrative support from the National Computing Centre.

Other sorts of user groups are built around users of similar systems rather than equipment. For example, finance officers in local authorities in Surrey meet as the Surrey Treasurers' Forum to compare policies and practices on the investment of capital and the workings of the money markets.

Groups of this kind are not the same as professional bodies (see Nos. 7 and 46), being more local and informal. And because they are usually relatively small user groups can also provide you with an opportunity to practise such skills as chairmanship and contribution to meetings, etc, in a more relaxed atmosphere than you may find in your professional body, where everyone tends to be more nervous of making mistakes in public.

# 46

# Actively Participate in your Professional Body

Whatever field of activity you work in, there will be an appropriate institute or association (see No. 7).

The majority of these bodies run a branch structure with regular meetings, and also produce newsletters. Some run an information service or library, which can give advice on tricky problems.

Most institutes welcome visitors and non-members who want to "test the water" before deciding whether to join. Make yourself known to one of the committee members.

If you decide to join, there are two main advantages of being an *active* member of your relevant institute:

1 By networking and picking other people's brains, you keep fresh and up to date in your occupation, which not only makes you more effective at work but also enhances your career prospects.

2 If you serve on a committee, become a branch secretary or fill a similar post, you will learn wider skills of negotiating, listening, influencing and organising which will stand you in very good stead. This is particularly relevant if your work is mainly technical and you are not responsible for staff. You may find yourself promoted to a post in charge of others almost overnight, and your "institute" experience will help you to tackle the challenge confidently.

# 47

# Develop a Network

Because the borderline between working life and home life is becoming increasingly blurred, it makes sense to develop contacts on both "sides" of the line. If you live in a traditional small village, you probably use a huge range of local contacts already; and when the village puts on its amateur dramatic society musical or organises the summer fête, all manner of talents and resources are mobilised.

In towns and cities, the organisations which are best known for networking across a range of occupations are Rotary, the Women's Institute and the Townswomen's Guild. Joining an organisation of this kind will provide opportunities for self-development that may not be available through membership of your own professional body (see No. 46) allowing you to draw on a wider range of experience and interests.

You could, for example, canvass fellow Rotarians to form an action-learning set (see No. 11).

Whether you live in a city or a village, the relevance of developing your personal "Mafia" is the same: you are enlarging the field within which your learning can take place. You are exploiting the learning opportunities that are available in all four quadrants of the diagram in No. 19.

## 48 Join a Support Group

Whereas a user group (see No. 45) is primarily focused on a special activity which you have in common with others, such as using the same computer system, a support group's main objective is your career development.

The best-known examples of support groups are those for women and for members of ethnic minority groups. The Pepperell Network, which was launched in 1992 with the aim of "opening doors to women's training and career options", now has approximately 1500 members. They hold regular meetings in various regional centres, and run training clinics on subjects such as managing your boss, creative thinking, coping with promotion and raising your profile.

Role-models are very important in support groups. Network members value the opportunity to ask people at first-hand how they manage to combine a career with a family, how they make decisions, what have been their formative influences, etc. Mentoring is another key activity.

The keys to success in a support group are that it must be run in a professional, non-patronising way, and should provide opportunities for genuine support. Members do not want glossy PR talks which evade the real problems, but practical help and encouragement, particularly during tough periods in their careers.

If a support group meets your needs, join and get involved. If one doesn't exist, get a few colleagues together and start one up for yourselves.

*Example:*

A district physiotherapist attended a Management Development Course for District Therapy Managers of the three professions; physiotherapy, occupational therapy and speech therapy. The 24 course members were allocated to three working groups of eight, with a mixture of these three professions. Her group got on well together and faced the same issues and problems, so they resolved to meet in the future as a support group. Four years on, they still meet about three-–four times a year to share their achievements and help resolve/advise on each others' problems.

The values of these meetings are numerous:

- Shared problems
- Sharing of information – no reinventing the wheel.
- Building on others' strengths and knowledge.
- In these times of rapid change it has proved a 'safety valve'.

## 49

# Coach your own Staff

It is very easy for us to consider ourselves "natural" coaches and to plunge in, albeit with the best intentions, showering some poor victim with an endless stream of advice. It happens in all areas of life, from learning to play golf to wallpapering the bedroom.

To be a good coach you do not necessarily have to possess the skill you are coaching. The coach of a high-jumper does not have to be a champion jumper, or even a mediocre one. The key lies rather in putting yourself in the learner's shoes and seeing the task as he/she sees it. If you are coaching me how to play Rachmaninov's Second Piano Concerto, the fact that you can play it blindfold from memory doesn't help me at all; what I need is help differentiating the white keys from the black keys.

So, in coaching you should remember:

- the learner's starting point may well be different from yours
- the learner's best route to the destination may be different from yours
- the learner's learning style (see No. 36) may be different: if you are a theorist and the learner is an activist, don't discourse at length or the learner will lose interest.

An excellent sequence for coaching is the GROW model, outlined in John Whitmore's book *Coaching for Performance* (see Resources section). You start by establishing a Goal for the learner – a specific, measurable level of performance that should be achieved after a specific period. Then consider the Reality – where is the learner starting from? What is he/she capable of now? Then move on to Options – review various possible routes to the goal. Finally, consider What is to be done – the detailed action plan.

Throughout the coaching process you are helping the learner, through questioning, to become more aware of his/her performance. Not so much "Why?", which makes the learner defensive, as "What?" and "How does it feel?" These questions allow you to see the task through the learner's eyes and enhance their ability to help themselves.

As a coach you are helping someone grow from dependence to independence. In the course of doing so, your own communication skills will improve, and you will come to appreciate the unique profile of each member of your team.

# 50

# Delegate Part of your Job

A very effective approach to delegation was generated by BICC, the electrical engineering company. In this system, if a manager has, say, five team leaders reporting to him/her, they together draw up a list of decisions which occur regularly in their department. These are grouped under headings such as finance, staffing, operations, etc. Alongside the list they draw up five columns, each headed by the name of a team leader. The manager then agrees a level of authority for each decision with each team leader. The possible levels are:

R – recommend: refer up to the manager

A – act: you have authority to decide without referring upwards

D – delegate: you have outgrown this decision and it ought to be handled by one of your team.

A single decision can be allocated different levels of authority according to the experience and skills of each team leader. For example, "Authorise overtime pay" might be labelled "R" for a new team leader and "A" for the other four; while "Alter delivery rota according to demand" might be labelled "R" for one person, "A" for three others and "D" for the most experienced team leader.

This system has several advantages:

- It ensures that everyone knows the extent of their authority.
- It provides a check on the work pattern of each person: looking down a team leader's column, is the balance right between "R", "A" and "D"?
- The intention is gradually to shift every decision from "Recommend" to "Act" and later "Delegate", so it provides a constant spur to the delegation process.

# Appendix

## Resources and Reading List

### A – Individual Study

*A practical approach to self development*
Tim Chapman, Training & Development, October 1992

*Individual Development Plans*
Charles Margerison, Management Development Review, Volume 5, No 4, 1992

*Managing Your Own Development*
David Turner, The Industrial Society

*Managing Yourself*
Video: Melrose

*Self Development*
David Megginson & Mike Pedler, McGraw-Hill, 1992

*Promoting the use of open learning: the open for learning initiative*
Employee Development Bulletin 56, August 1994

*Open learning hits its stride with multi media*
Sarah Hegarty, Works Management, March 1995

*The Learning Experience with Peter Honey*
Video: BBC in Business, 1992

*Organisations Learning to Succeed – Encouraging employees to learn and develop*
Video: BBC in Business

*How to develop and manage an open-learning scheme*
Roger Lewis, Council for Educational Technology, 1995

*Open Learning by PC or Paper?*
David Littlefield, Personnel Management, September 1994

*The Mind Map Book*
Tony Buzan with Barry Buzan, Wyvern Business Library, 1994

*Harnessing the Para Brain*
Tony Buzan, Wyvern Business Library, 1994

*Rapid Reading*
Janis Grummit, The Industrial Society

*Learning Log*, Peter Honey, 10 Linden Avenue, Maidenhead, Berks, SL6 4HG

Management Charter Initiative (MCI), Russell Square House, 10 Russell Square, London, WC1B 5BZ, (0171 872 9000)

National Council for Vocational Qualifications, 222 Euston Road, London, NW1 2BZ, (0171 387 9898)

## B – Group Work

*Managing Best Practice 11 – Self Managed Teams*
The Industrial Society, June 1995

*The Application of Action Learning: a practical guide*
George Boulden & Alan Lawlor, Management Development
Branch, ILO, Geneva

*Action Learning*
Krystyna Weinstein, Harper Collins, 1995
Contact: Centre for Action Learning Ltd, 43 Bainton Road,
Oxford OX2 7AG

*Team Leading – Becoming an effective team leader*
Video: BBC for Business, 1994

*The Wisdom of Teams*
Jon Katzenbach & Douglas Smith, Harvard Business School
Press, 1993

*Pulling together – teamwork in practice*
Alison Hardingham & Jenny Royal, Institute of Personnel &
Development, 1994

*Building the Perfect Team*
Video: Video Arts

*Selecting the Perfect Team*
Video: Video Arts

*The Administration Game Self Study Workbook*
The Industrial Society, 1994

*Outdoor Training for Employee Effectiveness*
Mark Tuson, Institute of Personnel Management, 1994

*A Checklist for using the Outdoors*
Steve Holman, Training Officer, Volume 31, No 2, March 1995

*Exercising Better Management Skills*
Donna Burnett, Personnel Management, January 1994

*Outdoor Management Development: insurance for the future*
Michelle Grant, Training Officer, Volume 31, No 2, March 1995

National Training and Consultancy Index, 25 Poland Street, London, W1V 3DB, (0171 494 0596)

*Leading Projects*, Trevor Young, The Industrial Society 1993

*The Motley Crew*, (teamwork video) Video Arts

*Handbook of Management Games*, Chris Elgood, Gower, 1993

*Action Learning in Practice*, Mike Pedler, Gower

TAPS (Training Access Points) – Local sources obtainable through your TEC (Training & Enterprise Council) or through National Training Information Central Support, Unit 4 AVEC 1 Sidney Street, Sheffield, S1 4RG, (0114 273 1883)

*Winning Teams* (video) The Industrial Society

*Short Cut to the Top*, Adrian Furnham, Financial Times, 13 January 1993

*Turn Management into an Adventure*, Philip Schofield, Sunday Times, 18 April 1993

*Risk in the Great Outdoors*, John Brank, The Independent on Sunday, 28 February 1993

*Teams Play Revealing Games*, David Guest, The Times, 11 February 1994

Contact: The Challengers Trophy, 30 Gordon Street, Glasgow G1 3PU, 0141 226 4454

## C – Change of Duties

*Sabbatical Leave*, IDS Study 506, May 1992

*Secondment & Employee Volunteering*, IDS Study 571, February 1995

*Born Again Secondment*, Widget Finn, Human Resources, March/April 1995

*Secondment – Volunteering to Improve Skills*, Catherine Dawson, Personnel Management Plus, April 1994

*High Fliers at TSB to be developed Using Secondments*, Personnel Management, August 1994, page 11

*Growing Your Own Managers*. The use of secondment in training and developing managers, Employment Department Group, HMSO, 1989

*A Practical Guide for Non-Executive Directors*, ProNed, 1 Kingsway, London, WC2B 6XF, 0171 240 8305

## D – Represent your Organisation or Colleagues

*Partnerships pass the 1,000 mark*, Personnel Management, April 1992

Business in The Community, 8 Stratton Street, London, W1X 5FD, 0171 629 1600

*Time Off for Trade Union Duties*, ACAS Code of Practice 3, HMSO

*Making Education Our Business*, Esso/DFEE/University of Warwick, 1995

*Managing Industrial Links*, David Warwick, The Industrial Society

*Industrial Twinning*, Ian Campbell & David John, The Industrial Society

*Safety Representatives and Safety Committees*, Health & Safety Commission

National Council of Voluntary Organisations, Regents Wharf, 8 All Saints Street, London, N1 9RL, 0717 713 6161

Charities Aid Foundation, 48 Pembury Road, Tonbridge, Kent, TN9 2JE, 01732 771 333

## E – Respond to Guidance

*Managing Best Practice 12 – Mentoring*
The Industrial Society, June 1995

*Mentoring*
Reg Hamilton, The Industrial Society

*The Manager's Guide to Counselling at Work*
Michael Reddy, British Psychological Society, 1993

*The Counselling Interview*
Video: Melrose

*The Empowering Appraisal*
Video: BBC for Business, 1993

*Marking the Managers: A guide to upward feedback*
Video: BBC for Business, 1994

*Being a protégé: a personal view!*
Croner, Issue No 374, 14 March 1994

*Criteria for successful mentoring*
Brian Willey, Croner, Issue no 373, March 1994

*Blooming Managers*
David Clutterbuck, Management Training, February 1994

*Mentoring Managers in Organisations*
Christopher Conway, Training & Development, December 1994

*Consenting Adults – making the most of mentoring,* (Video) – Channel 4 Television, and booklet

*Mentoring – the definitive workbook,* Ann Holloway, Development Processes (Publications) Ltd/Swansea College

*The Manual of Learning Styles,* Peter Honey, and Alan Mumford, published by Peter Honey

*Management Teams – why they succeed or fail,* Meredith Belbin, Butterworth-Heinemann

*TMS: The Personnel Development Manual,* Charles Margerison, Dick McCann, TMS Development International Ltd

For details of the Strength Deployment Inventory (SDI), contact Personal Strengths Publishing (UK) Ltd, 22 St Peter's Road, Oundle, Peterborough, PE8 4NS, (01832 272 429)

*The One Minute Manager,* Kenneth Blanchard and Spencer Johnson, Fontana

## F – Creative Skills

*Creative Thinking & Brainstorming*
Geoffrey Rawlinson, Gower, 1993

*The Blue Movie* – Generating Great Ideas
Video: Melrose

*Ideas into Action*
Video: Melrose

*Effective Business Reports* – The Write Stuff
The Industrial Society, 1993

*Report Writing* – The art of writing a good report
Video: Video Arts

*Oh What a Lovely Report*
Video: Longman Training

*Lateral Thinking*, Edward de Bono

*Creative Thinking*, Alan Barker, The Industrial Society, 1995

*Time and Workload Management*, Debra Allcock, The Industrial Society

*Leaders – The Learning Curve of Achievement*, Andrew Forrest and Patrick Tolfree, The Industrial Society

## G – Build up Contacts

*Networking & Mentoring* – A Woman's Guide
Dr Lily Segerman-Peck, Piatkus, 1991

For women's support groups, see the chapter on 'Networking' in *'Back to Work'* – a resource guide for women returners' by Gill Sargeant, The Industrial Society

# H – Develop Others

*The Coach*
Video: Melrose

*Coaching for Results*
Video: BBC For Business, 1993

*Coaching – Realising the Potential*
Paul Kalinauckas & Helen King, Institute of Personnel & Development, 1994

*Coaching for Performance*
John Whitmore, Nicholas Brealey Publishing, 1992

*How to be a Good Coach*
Tom Barry, Management Development Review, Volume 7, no 4, 1994

*Performance Coaching*
Trevor Bentley, Training Officer, Volume 31, no 2, March 1995

*Effective Delegation*
Video: Melrose

*101 Ways to Develop Your Staff Without Really Trying*, Peter Honey, McGraw Hill.